Madrid Revisited

MADRID REVISITED

Life and Labor in a New Mexican Mining Camp in the Years of the Great Depression

• •

RICHARD MELZER

The Lightning Tree—Jene Lyon, Publisher • Santa Fé, New Mexico

The author wishes to express his thanks and appreciation to the Huber family.

Cover Photograph by Paul Logsdon

Library of Congress Catalog Card Number:

76-18599

ISBN:

Paper Bound: 0-89016-024-4

Hard Cover: 0-89016-025-2

PRINTED IN THE UNITED STATES OF AMERICA

Second Printing 1984

THE LIGHTNING TREE—Jene Lyon, Publisher

P. O. Box 1837   Santa Fé, New Mexico 87504-1837   U.S.A.

For My Parents.

• Introduction •

MADRID, NEW MEXICO, was far better known for the color and bright lights of its Christmas displays than for the soot and clatter of its coal production in the 1930s. As many as 100,000 visitors a year came from all over the world to see this "Christmas City" of the Southwest. On a single evening 3,240 cars ventured the 45 miles from Albuquerque or the 25 miles from Santa Fe to see the famous winter celebration.[1] The caravan of vehicles stretched for miles over unpaved and often slippery roads. Madrid's Christmas became so elaborate and well-known that it received press coverage from as far away as New York and Trans-World Airlines rerouted several of its flights so that passengers could see the holiday spectacle from the air.[2]

The vast majority of visitors had only the most pleasant memories of Madrid, for a trip there at Christmas was, in one man's words, "just like you were going to heaven."[3] Many agreed with the editor of the *Albuquerque Journal* when he returned from Madrid and wrote that "In a world sadly overburdened with strife, contention, bigotry, [and] animosities of every degree, one may be glad that somewhere there is peace and contentment."[4] At least one visitor waxed poetic after his pilgrimage to the town and wrote:

> Russia's dictator, Stalin, has said
> " 'Tis well proven, God is Dead."
> Mussolini from Italia's sun kissed shore,
> Declares, "Religion is no more."
> German Hitler proclaims, in the name of Peace,
> That man's faith, in Faith, shall cease.
> But the lights of Madrid this message give,
> Religion, Faith, and God yet live.[5]

The town and its Christmas had become symbols of hope in a troubled society whose values and traditions were constantly challenged or ignored during the Great Depression.

But Madrid was criticized as well as applauded in the 1930s. Radical labor leaders found fault with everything from the conditions of the miners' shacks to the rate of wages paid in those hard times. In 1934, for example, one leader complained that Madrid was "an awfully bad place, [and] as bad as coal mining conditions were 44 years ago. . .they are just as bad in this camp now, and maybe worse."[6] These critics argued that only unionization and collective bargaining could rescue the miners from their miserable plight in a company town.

One must wonder if the situation in Madrid was either as good *or* as bad as contemporary observers would have us believe. Most of these commentators were outsiders who came to town in search of either peace and joy at Christmas or problems and strife to justify the creation of a labor union. Their reports may well be dismissed as self-fulfilling prophesies that shed more light on their authors' private interests in Madrid than on actual conditions during the Depression. It is the purpose of this book to sort out these distorted views and take a new, more historical look at life and labor in Madrid as uncovered in interviews with the people who lived there and the letters and records of the company that owned the famous little town. These several sources not only shed new light on the society of a single mining camp, but also reveal much about the impact of the Great Depression and New Deal on New Mexico as a whole.

Madrid Revisited

• 1 •

MADRID WAS, above all else, a company town. The Albuquerque & Cerrillos Coal Company operated and eventually owned the town's general store, hotel, barber shop, beauty parlor, car dealership, tavern, Amusement Hall, public utilities, hospital, athletic fields, houses, and, of course, the coal mines themselves. The firm and its representatives also dominated the government, the police, the school board and the credit facilities of Madrid. It is no exaggeration to state that the coal company's presence was felt in all places and at all times and, from 1919 to 1954, the company's enormous power was centered in the hands of a single individual: Oscar Huber. Although the business was owned by George Kaseman of Albuquerque until 1938, it was Oscar Huber who served as the superintendent and ruled Madrid, in his own words, as a "benevolent monarch."[7]

Oscar Huber was a short, bespectacled man who commanded the respect of even his worst enemies in the ranks of labor. According to these individuals, Huber was a "slick talker" who handled every situation with a "silk glove," but he was also a "good man" who was a gentleman to every lady, regardless of class.[8] Others called Huber a dictator, but quickly added that he was "fatherly" and "forthright" as well.[9] The superintendent was able to seem both manipulative and magnanimous because he was a master in the art of handling his workers and had definite ideas about what motivated their behavior. These ideas were often paternalistic and outdated, but they determined company policies and were clearly reflected in the labor relations and social life of Madrid.

Huber was, for example, a firm believer in the Protestant work ethic. According to the superintendent, idle time spawned trouble only if men could not channel their surplus energy into healthy, constructive activities. Huber realized that his employees had many hours of such idle time during the Depression when the coal market suffered and the mines were often worked only once or twice a week. Fearing that labor unrest might surface if the men had "plenty of time to grieve over their troubles," Huber promoted, supported and personally ran the Madrid Employees Club to reap "the intangible benefits of keeping our employees satisfied by keeping their minds occupied with wholesome entertainment."[10]

The Employees Club sponsored nearly every social activity in Madrid. The organization celebrated Easter, the Fourth of July, and, of course, Christmas with elaborate festivities that often took weeks and even months to prepare while keeping the men busy and, supposedly, content. The club also held raffles and dances, supported Madrid's baseball team and marching band and built athletic facilities that included a golf course in the hills west of town. Before the club was formed in the mid-1920s, Madrid's citizens had complained that there was little to do in town but drink at the tavern, play pool or stroll down the tracks with one's family on Sunday afternoons.[11] The Employees Club thus relieved the boredom and isolation of the coal camp and, Huber was convinced, kept the men too busy to think about their economic plight, listen to union organizers or attend union meetings in search of some other form of excitement.[12]

Madrid's Fourth of July was long billed as the greatest Independence Day celebration in all of New Mexico.[13] The Employees Club started planning for this holiday as early as April when the mining crews built ornate floats and hired acts to perform.[14] As many as six thousand visitors came from every part of the state to see the great spectacle. The town's festival featured a parade with up to 63 floats, a baseball game, a pie-eating contest, foot races, Indian dancers, cowboy singers, rodeo acts, wrestling matches, a street dance and half an hour of colorful fireworks display in the shapes of flags and other patriotic symbols.[15] Madrid's greatest Fourth of Julys were held in the decade 1922-32 but the town continued to celebrate the national holiday, albeit with less fanfare, all during the 1930s.

The coal camp's baseball team was likewise known throughout New Mexico and drew enormous crowds to witness its diamond wizardry. The Employees Club supported the powerful "Madrid Miners" by supplying uniforms and equipment, providing transportation to away games and building the first ball park in the state with a grandstand and electric scoreboard. The team won many a pennant in the Central New Mexico League and was manned by both miners and semi-professional athletes. The latter were usually adventuresome wanderers who never quite made it to the big leagues due either to their lack of talent or personal problems, such as old injuries or the lure of Demon Rum. The professionals were normally given rather easy jobs in camp and all players received bonuses after winning seasons. The miners never resented these privileges because they were enormously proud of Madrid's sports heroes and their exploits on the playing field. Dozens of workers watched the team practice each evening after they finished their shift in the mines. On Sundays the men parked their cars along the foul lines as early as 7 a.m. to reserve a place to see the afternoon game. At about noon, many families brought picnics to eat while they waited for the game to begin against such arch rivals as the Albuquerque Dons, the Santa Fe Clossons, the Las Vegas Maroons and the Bernalillo Lumberjacks. By the time the first ball was pitched Madrid was like a ghost town, for nearly everyone in the coal camp was at the game. Afterwards the miners talked for hours about disputed plays or the amazing pitching of E. J. "Chief" Bowles, the clutch hitting of Johnny "Red" García and the superb slugging of Harry "Pop" Stowers.[16]

Easter was celebrated in a much simpler fashion and for almost everyone but the children lacked the glamour and excitement of Madrid's Fourth of July or baseball season. The Employees Club distributed as many as 150 dozen eggs to the women in camp who boiled and colored them shortly before Easter Sunday. Several men would then hide the decorated eggs in the hills west of town, and on Easter morning the miners' children were driven out to the area in company trucks. When all was ready a gun blast signaled the start of Madrid's wild annual egg hunt. As many as 750 children swarmed over the hills in search of the colored eggs and the twelve wooden ones that were painted gold. These golden eggs were especially valuable, worth a dollar each to the lucky hunters who found them. But no one went home unrewarded. Every contestant received a bag of candy from the Employees Club on this spring holiday.[17]

The Fourth of July, the baseball team and Easter were all important Employees Club projects, but none of them ever challenged Christmas as the organization's major undertaking each year. Work on the Christmas project began in the early fall when Huber met with the Employees Club Board of Directors, which included all foremen and several loyal "company men."[18] These leaders discussed plans and suggested new ideas before each foreman's crew was assigned a specific task from the long list of jobs to be completed before December. The carpenter's crew might be expected to build new dioramas or repair old ones, while a crew of miners might be sent into the hills to cut down Christmas trees for the front lawn of every house in town.

This work was all volunteer labor that had to be done in the evenings or on weekends. Some men became genuinely interested in the annual project, while others either felt that the company expected them to work or simply welcomed the chance to escape from a house of unruly children.[19] Still others had to be induced to volunteer their time. More than one foreman had to promise his crew an abundant supply of beer or whiskey in order to get his men to finish their assigned task.[20] Many miners were understandably less than enthusiastic about offering their labor after a long day of digging and loading coal. Huber nevertheless reported that at least in 1931 many of the men who did the most work in the evenings "were miners and at times we actually had more help than we could use. . . .During these evenings a fine spirit prevailed and the men were all pleased with their accomplishment and were proud of the same."[21] The superintendent truly believed that all of his many efforts to keep his men busy and out of trouble were paying off, for there was little visible unrest in Madrid until 1933. As late as 1936 one citizen of the town testified that the Christmas "season takes our minds from our regular duties and is a great diversion."[22]

The entire village eventually became involved in the great project. Each year the Employees Club used as many as 50,000 lights, 20 miles of wire, two railroad cars of lumber, 75 gallons of paint, 6,000 square yards of canvas and 500,000 kilowatt-hours of electrical power.[23] The cost of these various supplies equaled three thousand dollars in 1940 and was paid for with both Employees Club and company funds.[24] The children decorated their school building, the Sunday School constructed the Nativity Scene, and at least one woman is said to have cut her long dark hair so that it could be used for Saint Joseph's beard.[25] The displays became more and more elaborate as sound systems and moving figures were added to the colored lights and decorations. All was ready by mid-December when the state's governor was often present to throw on the lights and officially open the Christmas season in New Mexico.[26] Witnessing this event in 1938, one reporter wrote that "Such words as colossal, stupendous, beautiful and amazing would fall short of [describing Madrid] at Christmas. Regardless of what words one uses, however, the lights of Madrid are undoubtedly one of the most beautiful tributes to Christmas and the spirit of the season to be found any place in the Christian world."[27]

The people of Madrid also celebrated Christmas in a more private, less spectacular fashion. Miners of Mexican descent, observing an old custom, burned cedar fires in the surrounding hills and *farolitos* on their roofs in order to light the path of the Christ Child.[28] When their displays were completed, all the men and their families were invited to a large "let down" dinner at the Lamb Hotel. And, as always, the children were never forgotten. Huber kept a census of all the children in town so that on Christmas morning each would receive a gift from the Employees Club. Men and women volunteers wrapped these gifts in the company store and as many as 800 children lined up to receive them in a row that stretched for nearly a mile down Madrid's main road. There would also be free rides and a picture show for the children as well as a dance for their elders on Christmas Day.[29] Everyone shared the joy of Madrid's holiday.

• 2 •

IT WOULD BE a serious mistake to argue that the purpose of these social activities was simply to pacify Madrid's impoverished workers in a program of welfare capitalism. Such a strategy was far too expensive, in terms of both time and money, unless the coal company could profit in yet other ways. Huber in fact had several additional ideas about how these activities could benefit his employees, their families and, above all, the Albuquerque & Cerrillos Coal Company.

First, Huber sought to create a proud and unified community in Madrid. The town's Christmas and other celebrations became unique customs that gave the small community a deep sense of identity and pride. The employees and their families read of their town in national magazines, saw thousands of visitors enjoy their annual festivities and wherever they traveled in New Mexico heard people talk of their athletic prowess. The cooperation needed in planning these activities unified Madrid's citizens in much the same way as barnraisings and cornhuskings once unified more rural communities. Finally, and no less importantly, the coal camp was united by its common sports heroes on the Madrid Miners. "Pop" Stowers and "Chief" Bowles played much the same role as such social heroes as "Babe" Ruth and "Dizzy" Dean played in America's larger urban centers. All these colorful men awed, inspired and united their fans in an otherwise drab and depressing decade.[30]

The coal company directly benefited from this strong sense of community pride. The firm needed a stable work force for its peak winter season, but the extreme difficulty of mining in the Ortiz Mountains discouraged many would-be employees. The veins of high grade coal dipped an awkward sixteen degrees into the earth and averaged only 3.5 feet in height.[31] Miners in Madrid had to labor with hand tools in small, wet and uncomfortable "rat holes," while those in Gallup and Raton found veins that were usually over six feet tall and far more accessible. Madrid's mines were not even worked consistently. Everyone in town listened intently at 5 p.m. each evening for the whistles that signaled if all or any of the mines would be worked on the following day.[32]

The Albuquerque & Cerrillos Coal Company was thus forced to compete for good workers and hoped that the social benefits of a well-developed community would help keep miners and their families in town. It was true that the men were often too poor to leave or too afraid they would not find work elsewhere, but the deep roots that many individuals had in the community were also responsible for Madrid's relatively stable population of about 275 employees. Huber was proud to state that "we strive to make the workmen satisfied with both their work and living conditions and I believe we are succeeding. Many of our employees have been with us ten years and more."[33]

Madrid's Employees Club activities had yet another important function for Huber and the coal company. The firm was always quick to point out that neither Christmas, the Fourth of July nor Easter were commercialized in Madrid for there were never any vendors in the street or admission fees to pay on these occasions.[34] The company nevertheless reaped large profits during the holiday seasons. In a highly revealing confidential letter to Kaseman, Huber explained how this profit was realized in July, 1931. The superintendent wrote that

> During the pre-celebration period our local people prepare in an unusual way and the [company] store does a much greater volume of business than usual. Our people stay home before the Fourth and get ready and after the Fourth because they are tired and have had all the excitement they want for some time, whereas if they left here to celebrate they would stay away until after all their money was spent. . . .We would [then] have to take care of them until they could again produce.[35]

Huber supplied statistics on company profits in order to prove his point. It was reported that Madrid's Lamb Hotel made $132.20 in June, 1931, and only $125.90 in August of that year, but took in $404.20 in the month of July alone. Profits in the Amusement Hall were even larger; while they totaled $131.29 in June and showed a net loss of $19.42 in August, they equaled $479.25 in July.[36] Business in these two enterprises thus improved over 330 percent in the short span of sixty days. If this was the size of the company's revenues during the summer holiday, one can well imagine the enormous profits realized at Christmas when the coal market was at its best, the miners had more money to spend and thousands of tourists (in need of food, drink and gasoline) motored through Madrid.

Perhaps most importantly, the coal company benefited from the great fame and glowing image of its small town. Madrid enjoyed a national reputation as a haven of peace and harmony at Christmas. Madrid's Independence Day, on the other hand, was recognized as a truly patriotic event in an age when Communists roamed the country and attacked American capitalism without mercy or respect. Meanwhile, the miners appeared to be enthusiastic, united and loyal baseball fans and their town "was about the best for good sportsmanship in the [Central New Mexico] league."[37] These were exactly the images of Madrid that the coal company sought to create for the public in New Mexico, the Southwest and, indeed, the nation. The firm was preoccupied with the town's image because it realized that if labor troubles ever plagued Madrid it would be extremely beneficial to have the public's sympathy on the company's side. Newspaper reporters, politicians and labor review boards might remember Madrid as a peaceful, patriotic and unified town where trouble could be caused only by outside radicals who were intent on destroying everything that was still good in America. The company also wanted to assure potential customers that Madrid was a peaceful community that could meet their demands for coal without the bothersome interruption of long labor strikes. Finally, Kaseman was concerned about his coal company's image of stability because he was the founder of the Albuquerque National Bank. The coal operator fully realized that trouble at Madrid might well shake the public's confidence in his growing bank during the financially insecure days of the Great Depression.[38]

The firm's interest in influencing public opinion was clearly reflected in the company's advertisements at Christmas. In December, 1937, the town's celebration was promoted in a full-page spread that appeared in the *New Mexico Magazine*. After cordially inviting the public to come see the camp's famous displays, the ad explained that

> In Madrid the Christmas spirit exists in every home and in every heart, for in addition to the visible illumination which gives this town its unusual and impressive Christmas atmosphere, there is another illumination which comes from the unseen lights of Joy, Hope and Peace which glow within us.[39]

Reporters continually emphasized this theme of contentment because this was what they heard from the company whenever they traveled to Madrid for feature stories. Fremont Kutnewsky visited the small town shortly after World War II but his experience there was typical of the previous decade. The writer and his wife were warmly received in Madrid on a quiet Sunday afternoon and talked with Huber for several hours without ever venturing far from the superintendent's front porch.[40] At the end of their limited visit Kutnewsky was nevertheless convinced that "There is more than a job here in Madrid to lure [miners]. There is a lovable home town—a town without government, but peaceful, homey and well-equipped for modern living."[41] Significantly, Kutnewsky's article did not mention nor did its author ever hear of labor unrest in Madrid.

Dozens of articles of the 1930s reveal this same naïvete. Three specific examples suggest the kind of information that the reading public received about conditions in the coal camp. In late 1936 Myrtle Andrews thus wrote that

> There is a feeling of conradery [sic] between the employees and employers [in Madrid]. At Christmas time the men are eager to take their turn at decorating after they have finished their shift of work, [for] none are ever too tired to do their share. . . .There is a happy light on the faces of. . .men [who] are called for special work, no matter how difficult.

Andrews completed her blissful picture by asking "What matters how much or how little Juan receives a month? His children will be treated the same as the children of his more fortunate neighbor [on Christmas]. What matters money today?"[42]

A correspondent for the *Albuquerque Journal* drew a similar conclusion after witnessing Madrid's Easter egg hunt. The reporter came to town after receiving an Employees Club invitation that was like "a request to appear at the Court of St. James." The telegram and egg hunt nevertheless produced the desired effect. The *Journal's* reporter soon wrote that Madrid "is more than a coal mining camp, it is a town where communal happiness is not only an advertised product, but a reality."[43]

Finally, on January 6, 1941, R. H. Faxon described Madrid's spectacular Christmas in the *Raton Daily Range*. This reporter wrote that "There has been a lot of flub-dub about how 'the poor miner is gyped' [sic] at Madrid. . . .To me, that is all bunk." Sixteen days later Faxon went so far as to write to Huber and declare that

> I shall never forget [Madrid's Christmas], and am treasuring my file of data [about it] to refer to, to write about occasionally, and to 'bat' anyone who, like our [labor leader] friend Mr. Hefferly. . ., seems inclined to criticise [sic], for any reason![44]

Huber and the coal company were extremely pleased with this kind of sympathy; it was like a holiday bonus rewarding their efforts to portray Madrid as a near-perfect community devoid of any real cause for labor unrest.

• 3 •

IF OSCAR HUBER believed that planned social activities would make his employees content in their spare hours, he felt more strongly that personal debts would make them produce more in their working hours. The miners were paid by the tons of coal they produced, but with numerous deductions from their wages, it was often difficult, if not impossible, for them to make ends meet. In January, 1940, for example, a miner listed the following deductions from his monthly pay:

$$\begin{array}{rl} \$\ 5.00 & \text{powder and fuse} \\ 1.50 & \text{mining lamp} \\ .75 & \text{Employees Club dues} \\ 18.00 & \text{rent} \\ \underline{3.50} & \text{coal (home fuel)} \\ \$28.75 & \text{Total} \end{array}$$

The miner's income averaged $50.00 per month in the winter of 1940, which left this individual less than $22.00 for his family's food and clothing for the next thirty days.[45] Many were unable to pay these essential bills and were therefore forced to see Oscar Huber and "draw scrip" against their future wages.

Scrip was a form of credit issued in company tokens or coins. The coal company justified its use by claiming that it was often unsafe to keep a large amount of cash in town, and that scrip was "only a convenient means of bookkeeping" for the office staff.[46] Huber also argued that if such credit were not extended to the men many of their families could not afford to eat and they would soon be added to the county welfare rolls. In addition, new employees had to be financed to "get them on their feet" so they could buy mining equipment and still manage to survive until their first payday in Madrid.[47]

While all of these explanations may well have been valid, it cannot be denied that Huber was able to employ this type of credit as a powerful weapon against his own men. He believed that men would work harder and produce more tons of coal if they were financially "in the hole" to the company. A system of industrial debt peonage soon developed. The superintendent went so far as to question certain men if they had not drawn credit for long periods of time.[48] Workers who seldom used scrip were often encouraged to buy luxury goods such as electrical appliances and new automobiles, so that they likewise would be in debt to the company.[49] By December, 1941, the *Albuquerque Tribune* could generously estimate that 90 percent of the men who had lived in Madrid for three or more years owned cars, while 95 percent owned radios, 75 percent owned washing machines and 50 percent owned electric refrigerators.[50]

According to Huber men would not only work harder but also remain in town longer if they continually owed money to their employer. However, during the Depression when money was scarce and job opportunities in other parts of New Mexico were even scarcer, the company did not have to advance very much credit in order to achieve this goal of keeping the men at work in the mines. Thus, as Figure 1 shows,

AVERAGE UNPAID OVERDRAFTS PER YEAR

	1916-19	1920-29	1930-39	1940-45
>$100	0	.7	.4	.5
$51-100	0	1.5	.9	4.6
$11-50	6.0	15.6	9.0	18.0
<$10	17.2	30.6	25.5	44.4

Source: Albuquerque and Cerrillos Coal Company Records

FIGURE 1.

fewer men with fewer debts left Madrid in the 1930s than in the generally more prosperous 1920s and early 1940s. This method of keeping men at work obviously had its pitfalls. Some debtors abandoned camp regardless of the state's economic situation, but compared to the total number of those who were saddled with debts and remained, the actual number of deserters was very small indeed. The Albuquerque & Cerrillos Coal Company gained far more than it lost through this strategic use of the scrip system.

The company benefited from its monopoly of the town's credit facilities in yet other ways, for the full value of scrip could be realized in Madrid's stores alone. The miners might use their tokens in neighboring Cerrillos or exchange them for hard cash, but only at a considerable loss. The discount rate on scrip varied from 15 to as high as 25 percent on the dollar in these years.[51] Armed with this enormous advantage, Huber seldom had to apply any great pressure to force his employees to trade in Madrid.

The men and their families were, moreover, well aware of the company's philosophy that if "You made your living in Madrid, . . .you were expected to spend your earnings there" as well.[52] Huber, in other words, felt that if the company was good enough to give a man a job and grant him some credit it was not too much to expect his loyalty and trade in return.[53] The company nevertheless resorted to more high-pressure salesmanship to convince certain men to buy expensive merchandise in Madrid. On at least one occasion a company man visited an employee and rather casually asked how many appliances the individual had in his home. Little more had to be said; the employee quickly recognized that the company wanted to see what he lacked in order to sell him more goods.[54] The worker ignored this particular "suggestion" and was never overtly penalized. But there was one indiscretion of this kind that was never tolerated by the company. If an individual ever planned to buy a new automobile he was expected to purchase it in Madrid or suffer dire consequences. One man had intended to buy a car in Albuquerque until he was approached by a foreman and told that "we can cut your work down" if the out-of-town purchase was not immediately cancelled.[55] The worker did not ignore the company's threat in this case because he realized the seriousness of the warning and had heard of men who were fired when they were foolish enough to commit this cardinal sin. As a car was the most expensive item that a miner could buy, Huber wanted to make sure it was bought in Madrid. The coal company could then profit not only by its actual sale but also by the increased production and longer tenure of the men who were burdened with this enormous debt.[56] Huber seldom had any problems selling his cars, however, for the company did not always require a down payment and owning an automobile became an important status symbol in Madrid. It was estimated that the community had the largest number of automobiles per capita in the entire state, although the miners could usually afford only enough gasoline to take short Sunday drives or ride up and down the main street of town in the evening hours.[57]

The scrip system was also employed as a powerful weapon against union activity in Madrid. Huber believed that when labor trouble threatened the coal company, financial credit could be used as both a carrot and a stick. In the fall of 1933 the superintendent wrote that "I have been more than usually liberal in the issuance of credit where I thought it would do good and keep individuals satisfied, for our discontent outside the [union] leadership is with those whose earnings have been quite low."[58] This tactic did not always produce the desired results, and the company was capable of reversing its policy when confronted with labor unrest. A union leader thus described conditions prior to and during a strike in 1934 by reporting that "The suffering recently has been acute. Credit at the company store has been cut off for many. Children are hungry and barefoot. Many miners cannot afford to take lunches into the mine, but drink only water at the noon hour."[59] It is impossible to say what ended this short strike, but Huber's denial of credit, when no other sources of aid were available, may have been a major factor in the miners' decision to return to work. As always, the coal company had its way when the situation was most critical in the decade of the Great Depression.

• 4 •

THOUGH THE COAL company may have dominated every important situation, it seldom did so without considerable opposition from the ranks of labor. Several unions vied for recognition and criticized the company after 1933 when the federal government appeared to condone labor activity in Section 7A of the National Industrial Recovery Act. In this famous clause the Roosevelt Administration sought to improve the status of labor in order to (1) increase the group's purchasing power by raising its wages, (2) assure labor's cooperation in the great plan for economic recovery and (3) rally the workers' political support for the future. Section 7A thus guaranteed labor's right to unionize, bargain collectively and obtain better working conditions in the 1930s.[60]

The important new law opened a floodgate of union activity in the country and it was not long before even small and isolated Madrid felt the impact of this great force.[61] Needless to say, the Albuquerque & Cerrillos Coal Company feared and opposed this liberal trend and, like many other businesses in the United States, it attempted to take the initiative in the coming industrial war. The firm thus organized a company union in the very same month that the National Industrial Recovery Act was passed into law. Madrid's organization and its program, known as the "Employees' Representation Plan," was supported by loyal company men who generally shared Huber's misgivings about labor radicals. The latter were stereotyped as "Old Mexican Mexicans" and outsiders that "stirred up lots of trouble."[62] Those in the company union sought to use only peaceful methods to attain limited goals. In November, 1933, the group reported that "We have asked [the coal company] for a number of things and some concessions have been granted and [we] believe more will be granted later. . . .Up to date we are reasonably well satisfied with conditions."[63] The farce of the company union did not last long, however, as its true nature was apparent to even the newest employees. They realized, as did the *Albuquerque Tribune,* that "At its best the company union is benevolent paternalism. At its worst it is a weapon for intimidation. It is in all cases a caricature of the real collective bargaining provided by [Section 7A of the NIRA]."[64]

The weak company union was all but forgotten when other, more radical groups sent organizers to Madrid in the second half of 1933 and in early 1934. The National Miners Union sent several of its representatives from the coal fields of McKinley County where the leftist union had been leading a long and often violent strike.[65] On November 2, 1933, "fiery" Martha Roberts "invaded" Madrid with a "flying squad" of radical followers and attempted to organize an NMU local. The group distributed union literature and held a meeting to rally support and advise the miners of the possible demands they could present to the company.[66] A local NMU chapter was organized in November, 1933. Sixteen demands were presented to Huber but it seems that Martha Roberts and her colleagues were far more interested in gaining Madrid's support than in solving Madrid's problems. Huber agreed to only eleven of the sixteen demands and refused to recognize the new union as the miners' bargaining agent. However, there was little serious talk of a strike at this time.[67] Instead, local leaders were busy raising money to support the strike in Gallup and writing a petition to the governor to win a pardon for Robert F. Roberts, who had been jailed for his union activities in McKinley County.[68] The miners of Madrid were not overly enthusiastic about Gallup's struggle, and when the NMU was discredited as "a bunch of Reds" supported by Russia, the local union lost nearly all of its power and influence in the camp.[69]

Local labor leaders were hardly discouraged by this initial failure. By the spring of 1934, Bill Zurek, Jesus Pallares and Tom Theopholis had organized a new United Mine Workers union. They promised to fight for the men "with the Government on their side," for with John L. Lewis on the National Labor Board the federal government appeared to recognize the UMW as the miners' sole representative in the country.[70] Though the town's UMW local was to lead four strikes during the next two years, none was very long and few were very violent.[71] The history of Madrid's Local 6920 was, in fact, marked by deep frustration and only limited success. There were many reasons for this disappointing situation which help to explain as much about life in Madrid as about the failure of the town's union in the mid-1930s.

It is important first to consider the nature of the complaints that caused unrest in Madrid. Labor leaders protested that the coal company refused to (1) recognize their union as the miners' bargaining agent, (2) negotiate in good faith, (3) sign a contract to increase wages and limit working hours or (4) allow the union to "checkoff" or deduct union dues from every miner's pay. Labor also objected to more specific problems in Madrid such as the Employees Club, the poor condition of housing, the high cost of living and the presence of a brutal company guard.

Huber had hired a new company guard in April, 1935. The man was known only as "Davis" but it was rumored that he had been a Southern prison guard who never brought an escaped convict back alive.[72] His rough treatment of drunks and street fighters was apparently tolerated in Madrid until early 1936 when Bill Zurek accused Davis of "mistreating members of our union, [and] beating them up when making arrests."[73] A strike was finally called when Zurek bitterly complained that the policeman was following him everywhere and interfering with his work as the union's checkweighman.[74] Those who walked out also demanded that the company sign a contract with the UMW local. The strike lasted one month, but company records show that the miners were seriously divided over the issues at stake. At least half the men either remained at work or signed a petition against the walk-out.[75] The strike ended on March 2, 1936, without Davis being fired or a contract being signed. An uneasy peace returned to Madrid.

The miners were also divided in opinion on the costs and benefits of the Employees Club. Union leaders often called volunteer work for the Employees Club "forced labor" and spread rumors that the company discharged individuals who were not always willing to offer their spare time and energy.[76] Others criticized the collection of club dues and called it a "racket" that profited the coal company far more than the men themselves. These dues were assessed according to one's income and averaged 75¢ per month, but the union complained that the collected funds were never accounted for since no one was allowed to examine the club's ledgers.[77] Some men lamented this added expense and wondered "What a lot of food and clothes that $9 would have bought, that $9 that had to go to help pay for these pretty lights. Could have used some of that money to buy something else besides beans for Christmas dinner."[78] According to Pedro Septulvida, the only way that Madrid's Christmas celebration really benefited the men was by "giving us more light at night."[79] It was argued that the Employees Club treasury could be far better utilized if it served as an emergency relief fund during the hardest days of the Depression.[80] Such measures were never attempted, but some workers continued to protest by circulating petitions, quitting the club, or on at least one occasion posting a large sign in the company store that read:

No more checking off 75¢ for Employees Fund. Don't
let them give us Christmas presents with our own money.[81]

Top: Miners at the end of a shift. No photographs of men at work in the mines were found, perhaps because the tunnels at Madrid were extremely low, making picture-taking difficult. *Bottom:* Madrid in the early 1970s. The Amusement Hall with the church directly above it is at left center; the company store and mine office at right center.

Overleaf: Madrid during the Depression years. Note the piles of coal in the miners' yards, which the company forced them to buy. The City of Bethlehem is in upper center. (Photographs from the Huber Papers.)

Fire, either in the mines or the town, was a dreaded event. Water was always in short supply in Madrid. It was often necessary to haul it in by tank cars when fire did occur. Building fires were usually extinguished with dynamite. (Photograph from the Huber Papers.)

The company store sometime in the 30s. Almost everything needed by the residents was available here. The quality of goods was high and so were the prices. (Photograph from the Huber Papers.)

Top: Left, George Kaseman. Right, Oscar Huber. Kaseman, long-time owner of the Albuquerque & Cerrillos Coal Company, died in 1938. Oscar Huber subsequently acquired ownership of the mines and the town. Huber died in 1962. (Kaseman photograph courtesy of the Albuquerque National Bank; Huber photograph from the Huber Papers.) Lower: The miners' shacks had been moved to Madrid around the turn of the century. They were cut into sections and hauled in on freight cars. The cracks were never adequately sealed. (Photograph from the McKittrick Papers.)

But most men seemed either satisfied or complacent about the Employees Club.[82] Few actually quit the group and the sign of protest in the company store was torn down in a few hours. Huber claimed that many of the names that appeared on petitions were forgeries or belonged to individuals who were paying little if any dues.[83] The Employees Club thus survived, despite criticism, as division again plagued all forms of protest engineered by the labor leaders of Madrid.

Local 6920 objected to the poor condition and high cost of housing as well. Most of the miners' houses had been moved to Madrid by cutting them into sections and transporting them on flatcars soon after the turn of the century.[84] In the 1930s families still complained about wall holes caused by this moving process. They argued that if you "could throw a cat through the cracks" before World War I, you could also find piles of snow in your rooms during the winter months of the Depression.[85] These "broken-down, draughty, and leaky houses" seldom had indoor plumbing or outdoor sewer connections.[86] Water had to be carried from a pump four to eight hundred feet away from one's home.[87] Water shortages were not unusual in this arid region and fires were a constant danger to Madrid's frame houses.[88] Rents were said to be too high, housing was often scarce and the men were charged for a ton of coal each month whether they needed it or not.[89] Piles of surplus coal cluttered the miners' yards, and many agreed with a worker who wished "I could resell some of that coal. I don't need it all, but I'd get fired if I did that."[90] There is no record of any man actually losing his job in this way, but the great fear of that possibility hung like the Sword of Damocles over the miners' heads and became an unspoken means of control for the coal company.

Huber and several other citizens of Madrid defended the level of rent and quality of housing almost as ardently as the union attacked them. These people argued that if some of the houses were in disrepair, it was often due to the individual tenant's carelessness and lack of initiative in fixing small things on his own.[91] The company was willing to supply paint and equipment for such repairs and a carpenters crew could be called in for larger jobs, such as roofing or the renovation of older homes. [92] A whole new section of town, commonly known as "Hollywood," was built to alleviate the housing shortage, and when homes burned down they were replaced with better, more modern buildings. Unlike many other coal camps, garbage was collected regularly, more and more houses had indoor plumbing and every house was wired for electricity.[93] Finally, the company went to some length to show that the cost of housing and public utilities in Madrid was competitive with similar costs in other company towns of New Mexico. According to these statistics only one such town in McKinley County had lower costs than Madrid. (Figure 2.)

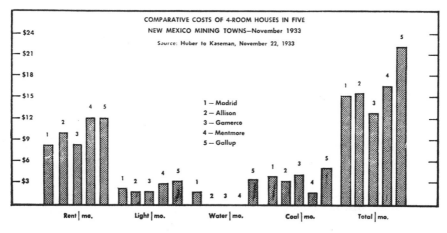

FIGURE 2.

Huber likewise boasted of the public school and medical facilities in town. One elementary school teacher, Julia Vergalio Weeks, had to learn five languages in order to teach her young immigrant charges to read and write in English, but she was usually successful in the difficult task. Madrid's institution became a model school in Santa Fe County.[94] The town also had a small hospital in the 1930s, and for only one dollar a month the company doctor treated all "ailments" except syphilis, pregnancy and injuries suffered in street fights. While other companies cared only for their immediate employees, the company in Madrid provided medical attention for the miners' entire families.[95]

This defense seemed most convincing but it contained several serious flaws. The cost of housing in Madrid may have compared favorably with McKinley County, but the company offered no information about prices in the coal towns of Colfax County. Moreover, while the cost of housing in Madrid remained relatively stable, the miners' average wages for an eight-hour day decreased by 31.2 percent from June, 1931, to October, 1935.[96] This meant that if a miner used 10.1 percent of his monthly income to pay for a four-room house in 1931, he had to pay 15.9 percent of his wages for the same unit only four years later. It is also interesting to note that most of those who defended Madrid's housing were loyal employees who lived on the front, or main, street of town, where the very best houses stood. The "front row" had a well-lit, smooth street and a wooden sidewalk; its buildings had most of the indoor plumbing, the strongest walls and the most efficient heating facilities in town.[97] The "best citizens" lived on this "silk stocking row" where one had to "sell his mind and soul" to the company in order to remain.[98] It is only natural that those who lived in these improved conditions have only the best memories of the homes, the school and the hospital in Madrid.[99]

The citizens of Madrid were again divided on the question of the company store. All agreed that families could buy almost anything in the town's store and that the quality of merchandise was usually excellent.[100] The union argued, however, that the price of goods was exorbitant considering the economic plight of the workers. Jesus Pallares insisted that "It is not exaggerating to state that the company is in the real estate and grocery business rather than the coal business."[101] The firm was accused of driving up the price of goods because it knew that the men could only use their scrip in town and because, in one miner's words, "There ain't no competition."[102] A survey of nineteen food items, ranging from pinto beans to tomato soup, revealed that the company did in fact enjoy a rather wide profit margin even considering the extra cost of freight charges to isolated Madrid. The selling price of these goods in 1939 was found to be 28.8 percent higher than their retail value.[103] These food prices were generally greater than those found in nearby Cerrillos or Santa Fe,[104] but they were competitive with, if not lower than, prices in Albuquerque. Grocery bills calculated from sales ads suggest that Madrid's regular prices were actually less than Albuquerque's in 1931 and 1935.[105] If a miner had cash rather than scrip, and had enough money to afford gasoline, he could save money by trading in Cerrillos or Santa Fe, if not Albuquerque. Since most men did not enjoy these advantages, they were forced by circumstances to pay the high cost of goods in Madrid.

The first reason for the failure of organized labor in Madrid therefore involved differences in opinion on such major issues as the type of union desired, the charge of police brutality, the benefits of the Employees Club, the condition and cost of housing and the price of merchandise at the company store. Every form of labor protest proved fruitless, as the miners were continually divided among themselves.

Another reason for labor's failure in the 1930s involved the miners' attitudes about unions in general. Many men distrusted the unions because they suspected that labor leaders were interested in outside struggles, personal ambition or monetary rewards rather than the specific problems of Madrid. Bill Zurek, the president of Local 6920, openly admitted "that he had to stay [in Madrid] until the contract was fixed up, after which he would probably get a better [union] job [elsewhere]."[106] Some individuals also believed that Zurek was receiving extra money either from the UMW or the coal company, for he seemed better off than most miners even after he became the union's checkweighman. A surviving thread of evidence seems to support this charge: in January, 1935, Huber's chief clerk reported that "I told Zurek a few days ago that we were falling behind. . .in the soft coal and he has arranged to change [the] scales again to catch up."[107] Zurek continued his labor activities despite this "arrangement," but regional labor leaders often offered to remove this thorn from Huber's side if the superintendent would simply sign a UMW contract.[108] Huber steadfastly refused. Many miners nevertheless learned of these and other irregular practices and eventually concluded that the unions indeed had a "racket," as Huber, Kaseman, the *Santa Fe New Mexican* and other conservative forces in the state had always claimed.[109]

Some miners also accused labor leaders of using intimidation and blatant lies in their efforts to control the camp. During one strike in 1936, a UMW official let it be known that union members would remember the blacklegs "for a long time in the future and pay them back with plenty of interest."[110] In April, 1936, miners from Alabama were also told that they would be blacklisted in union-dominated coal fields back home if they refused to join the local in Madrid.[111] Later, in 1939, Huber wrote that union representatives were "pestering" the men to sign up with the UMW and some workers joined simply "to get rid of them. Also we have had some cases of our men being threatened if they do not sign."[112] Miners became even more disillusioned with the unions when labor leaders "promised us the moon" but seldom delivered even modest improvements.[113] At the conclusion of the February, 1936, strike UMW leaders went so far as to claim victory and instruct the miners to return to work because Huber was about to sign a contract. The superintendent reported to Kaseman that he never made such a promise,[114] and in all of the 1930s no union was ever able to negotiate a contract with the coal company. By July, 1937, Local 6920 was almost entirely discredited. As one Mexican miner explained, "all the men here are afraid to sign up with the union as they have been double crossed and badly beaten in the last attempt they made to organize and strike at this place [in February, 1936]."[115]

The final and most important reason for the failure of organized labor involved the power and tactics of the coal company itself. All other causes can, in fact, be traced back to this single factor. The company had always done as much as possible to keep the miners divided while it discredited the unions and their leaders in a long propaganda campaign. Huber and Kaseman were successful in these efforts because they employed every weapon at their command, doing so with a practiced skill that separated them from most other business leaders in their state and in their age.

The coal operator and his superintendent developed their skill in handling labor through careful observation and patient planning. The two men communicated in letters and coded telegrams at least once a day from mid-1933, when the NIRA was enacted, to mid-1938, when Kaseman was killed in an oil explosion near Hobbs, New Mexico.[116] Their correspondence reads like the communiques sent between a field general and his headquarters; no detail was neglected in this pitched war against labor.

The coal company gathered information about its enemy through a well-developed intelligence system. Huber learned much, for example, through the "washhouse grapevine," where rumors often started as the men cleaned up after their shifts in the mines. But the superintendent, seldom satisfied with this source of information alone, enlisted a squad of informers to attend union meetings and report on every speech and decision made behind closed doors. Unlike other managers Huber even allowed these meetings to be held on company property—in Madrid's Amusement Hall or at its baseball park. The men did not have to meet along deserted country roads as they were forced to do elsewhere; Huber was anxious to keep the unions' sessions close to home where he could scrutinize events or send "friends of the company" to do so for him.[117]

These "friends" also reported to Huber when suspicious newcomers were seen in town. Dale Darling, who ran Madrid's Lamb Hotel, thus spotted four strangers registering for rooms in August, 1933. The innkeeper donned a pair of overalls to appear as a miner and, after listening to his guests' conversation, quickly alerted the mining office that these men were undoubtedly radicals who were up to no good in town. The four were carefully watched until they retreated from Madrid in a few days.[118]

Huber gathered much of his information on his own as well. The superintendent was a "slick talker" and learned many things during either casual interviews with miners or formal meetings with labor leaders.[119] The latter negotiations often lasted long into the night, for Huber debated every issue like a Philadelphia lawyer. The superintendent was nevertheless convinced that

> considerable good has been accomplished thru these confer-
> ences. We have been able to get all the facts pertaining to our
> situation before the outside leaders [do, while]...our local
> people...have also become acquainted with our [business]
> conditions...which they knew nothing about before these con-
> ferences [began].[120]

Labor-management negotiations had become a clever cover for the
company's information gathering, although they seldom benefited the
workers and never produced a union contract in the 1930s.

Huber's devious methods did not stop here. The company was not
above intercepting union telegrams, opening private letters, sending
spies to check on strangers in neighboring Cerrillos or writing to state
agencies for information about unfamiliar cars parked in Madrid.[121] Huber also met with other coal operators to exchange notes on union activity, had his chief clerk report on the radio news of serious strikes in
New Mexico and received intelligence from men who traveled through
the coal fields of the Southwest.[122] The result of this enormous effort
was that Huber and Kaseman generally knew so much about labor's
thinking and plans that the coal company was usually several moves
ahead of its adversaries in every dispute. The firm could therefore hope
to frustrate union demands, avoid crises and prevent great violence. It
often seemed that labor's battles were lost before they began for the
company was in control of almost every difficult situation that raised
its troublesome head.

Huber used his collected information to prevent crises in more
subtle and less violent ways than most superintendents. While others
fired, evicted, coerced or pressed legal charges against union leaders,
Huber realized that such direct measures could only antagonize workers and create martyrs in the ranks of labor. Madrid's superintendent
did employ rather harsh techniques, but he made sure they were cam-
ouflaged as much as possible so that he could at least claim that "No
one has ever been punished by this company for union activities."[123] In
May, 1934, Huber laid off three miners, including two union men, but
used the excuse that "in order to give the men who stayed more work
it was necessary to lay off some. . . .We laid off the most inefficient first,
which was only natural."[124] On another occasion the company evicted
the local union's vice-president, Jesus Pallares, but was extremely careful to act on the legal grounds that the miner was not paying his
rent.[125] Finally, in July, 1935, Bill Zurek accused Huber of cutting off

the electricity in his house for six days as "another damfool trick" to get rid of him.[126]

The company also used third parties to punish its enemies in order to avoid the responsibility for such acts. Huber and Kaseman thus cooperated with immigration officers in order to deport foreign agitators[127] and collected the criminal records of labor leaders in case such information could be used against these distrusted individuals.[128] In January, 1936, for instance, a union leader dynamited explosives in a mine still occupied with men, but Huber refused to press charges because "it would only stir up commotion. . .and. . .having this hanging over [the leader's] head might make him behave somewhat better."[129] Employing a similar tactic Huber once wired the sheriff in Cerrillos that two of his deputies had been seen on a Madrid picket line. Within two hours Sheriff Romolo Lopez reported that he had contacted his men and told them "to stop from interfering in the Madrid situation or their commissions will be cancelled."[130] The deputies were never seen on Madrid's picket lines again. And in at least one case the company "brought considerable pressure" on a worker whose son made trouble through the union, although the father was "a trusted employee" and "all right in every respect."[131]

The coal company also averted trouble with more preventive measures. Kaseman warned his superintendent to "try to keep people out of camp unless they have very definite business there."[132] Although Madrid was never fenced in and guarded as some camps were, strangers were carefully watched and sometimes "kicked down the canyon" if they disturbed the peace in any way. Huber was equally careful in hiring new workers when there was labor trouble in other parts of New Mexico; these strangers might spread the unrest to Madrid and add strength to the radical minority in town.[133] A surplus of coal functioned as yet another obstacle to labor trouble. Huber explained that extra coal "'serves two purposes (one) to prevent a strike and (two) to take care of our customers, if we have a [strike]."[134] Union leaders who realized that the company could meet its business demands during a long walkout would be less likely to take the risk of stopping work in the mines.[135] In the late summer of 1935 a county welfare agent found that Madrid's hard-coal miners were working more than usual and that the coal cars at Waldo and Madrid were "filled to capacity" because in the previous months there had often been talk of strikes.[136] The miners recognized this ploy but desperately needed the work during the off-season summer months. The scheme apparently worked; two years later Huber could still argue that "there is no better insurance to prevent. . .

trouble than a good supply of coal on the tracks."[137]

But the company's greatest weapon against labor was Oscar Huber himself. Unlike the employees of larger companies, Madrid's workers could deal with their employer on a close personal basis. Huber's long tenure, moreover, provided continuity to both his policies and his relations with the men. The superintendent claimed that his office door was open to all, but those who had the nerve to take this opportunity usually met their match. Huber could negotiate with any miner, union official, labor board or state governor and still remain unscathed.

Huber defended his company against the unions by arguing that the firm was losing money in Madrid and could simply not afford to increase wages or plan major reforms. He argued that both the Depression and competition from more modern fuels such as natural gas and oil had caused net losses for the coal company in four of the last six years of the 1930s.[138] Union members, he continued, represented only a minority of his employees and were known as the "bad actors" of Madrid.[139] The superintendent claimed that these miners were usually of Mexican descent, poor citizens and lazy workers who could never be satisfied. Their leaders were described as outsiders and Communists, who were interested in Madrid only as a place to operate a lucrative "racket."[140]

Huber supplied a great mass of data to "prove" these accusations. Shortly after the strike of February, 1936, for example, he reported that each man who had picketed produced an average of 10.50 tons of coal in the second week back at work, while those who had not picketed mined an average of 19.16 tons in the same period.[141] Huber, however, did not mention that the strikers suffered some major disadvantages in this competition because (1) they had to clean up their old rooms in the mines or be assigned new places before they could begin to produce again and (2) only the production of 43 non-strikers was reported, although these men may or may not have been typical of the more than 80 men who did not choose to picket in Madrid.

The superintendent's statistics on the strikers' citizenship abilities were likewise faulty. After checking the poll books from the general election of November, 1934, Huber discovered that of Madrid's 421 voters, 205 worked during the February, 1935, strike, while only 88 were seen on the picket lines.[142] The superintendent concluded that the loyal workers were far better citizens than the "shiftless" strikers. The great problem with this mode of reasoning is that although the number of men who worked and the number of men who struck were almost equal, the percentage of those who picketed and were U. S. citizens was only about 33 percent. There were thus many more non-strikers than strikers who were able to exercise the right to vote. A simple calculation in fact reveals that the percentage of those citizens on the picket line who did vote was about equal to the percentage of those citizens who voted and still worked during the month of February. If Huber's figures reveal anything it is that the U. S. citizens who struck fulfilled their civic responsibility to vote *just as well as* their peers who chose to remain in the mines.

Despite the biased flaws in its reasoning the coal company continued to have the upper hand in most of its dealings with labor. By controlling all credit, keeping the men divided, gathering all the information it could, anticipating labor's moves, involving third parties to threaten its enemies and employing the force of Huber's personality, the company was continually able to strike the main blow against organized labor in Madrid. Thus, while the unions fought with renewed strength and slightly greater success during World War II, their history was filled only with disappointment, disillusionment and repeated defeats in the years of the Depression.

• 5 •

IF THE UNIONS were ineffective, prices high, wages low and work scarce in Madrid, one must wonder how most miners and their families managed to survive through the 1930s. Scrip, of course, provided some relief, though it buried the men in debts that often took years to repay. Whenever possible, miners turned to alternate sources of income. Some worked as farm laborers in the summer while other, more adventuresome men mined for gold in the hills south of town.[143] No one ever made a fortune in gold, however, and few made as much as four dollars a day by selling their precious nuggets to the company store.[144] The poorest families meanwhile applied for county welfare when it was made available. Welfare rolls swelled in the summer months when the coal business declined and money was rare in town. A county welfare agent reported that in March, 1935, there were 26 households on relief, while only four months later there were almost three times as many families that required these emergency funds.[145] Santa Fe County sometimes provided groceries as well, while the federal government occasionally slaughtered cattle and distributed the meat to the very poorest families in town.[146]

Huber considered direct relief a "bad thing" that only encouraged lazy workers to strike while they enjoyed outside aid.[147] Direct relief in fact created laziness in men, according to Huber, because when "their living [is] so well assured from relief sources...men don't look for work. They probably hang around a locality where there is no work" just to be able to collect welfare.[148] The superintendent thus sought state and federal work-relief projects that might benefit poor miners but not produce laziness or endanger the coal company. A "sewing... and an outdoor project" were created in the spring of 1935[149] and a WPA program was established in the late 1930s. Those involved in the latter project built a new stone-walled school with company support.[150] Some individuals fastidiously claimed that the letters WPA stood for "We Putter Along,"[151] but Madrid's project more than fulfilled its function as the miners received needed cash for their labors, the community enjoyed enlarged educational facilities and many workers who might have left or struck remained in town and spent their new income in the company store.

Life, then, was a constant struggle for the miners of Madrid. It is therefore surprising that despite the poverty, the company's machinations and the unions' failures, most former citizens of the town remember the 1930s as the best years of their lives. Regardless of their social class they recall the unity created by Employees Club activities far more than the division caused by the town's few short strikes. They recall the camp's social and racial equality far more than the fact that 70 percent of the miners were of Mexican descent, 15 percent Anglo-American, 10 percent Slavic or Italian and about 5 percent Black.[152] "No one felt better or worse than anyone else" because the majority of miners lived in similar houses, worked at similar jobs, had similar belongings and suffered similar deprivations.[153] And, finally, the miners recall Huber's benevolent paternalism far more than his manipulation of all affairs. Few realize that *both* the coal company and the labor union ran "rackets" at the miners' expense in Madrid.

The human mind has a propensity to remember the best times and forget the painful past, but when so many individuals agree, their judgement cannot be ignored. Though life in Madrid was difficult and labor in the mines was often dangerous, it is generally remembered as a happy, simple existence in an isolated, small-town environment. The old town is still mourned by the people who worked, played and suffered there in the years of the Great Depression. The lights of Madrid will shine in their hearts forever.

• 6 •

IT IS IRONIC that after many long years of depression only war, with all its horror and death, could breathe new life into the American economy. The war industry of the early 1940s spawned more jobs, higher wages and greater opportunities in New Mexico and the nation.

Madrid shared in this renewed prosperity if only for a fleeting moment. By November, 1941, the *Santa Fe New Mexican* reported that "the miners' pockets are jingling with [their] greatest earnings since the [First] World War."[154] In that same month Oscar Huber claimed that his company's "Production has increased 25 percent. . .and we have 15 percent more employees" than in 1940.[155] The miners now worked consistently, for it was not long after Pearl Harbor that Huber secured a contract to supply all the coal needed for the new scientific community at Los Alamos. Coal was used at Los Alamos because there had not been enough time, labor or material to lay gas pipes to the secret site in the mountains. Huber's fleet of fifteen trucks made countless trips up the steep road to Los Alamos, although Madrid's miners had little idea where their coal was destined or how it contributed to the making of the atomic bomb. An average of one hundred tons of coal was brought to Los Alamos each day, while smaller amounts were shipped to less strategic war industries of the American Southwest.[156]

Madrid's coal was thus in great demand during World War II, but the Albuquerque & Cerrillos Coal Company soon found it increasingly difficult to satisfy its business orders. Many young men went off to fight overseas while others moved on in search of higher wages than Huber could offer. The lure of "Golden California" with its defense plants and modern society drew growing numbers from small and isolated Madrid.[157] The State Mine Inspector of New Mexico discovered that although 216 men were employed as miners in Santa Fe County in 1941, only 161 were left in 1943, and a scarce 82 remained in early 1945.[158] As many as 30 families were said to have abandoned Madrid on a single day as the war raged overseas.[159]

This steady migration from town only increased with the news of peace in 1945. The coal company suddenly lost its previously firm control over the miners and their lives. The Employees Club, for example, hardly functioned after the war and did little to make Madrid a unified and proud community.[160] The miners' shacks were in growing need of repair as there were fewer and fewer men to spare for such odd jobs in town. One miner, Manuel García, declared that in these declining years "you could break your leg on a broken stoop before the company would fix it."[161] At last, many who had mined simply to avoid the draft quit their jobs as soon as peace was won in the Pacific. On V-J Day in 1945 over one hundred employees resigned and joined the exodus from town.[162]

Not even exorbitant debts could keep miners in Madrid any longer. The men would sooner leave the expensive goods they had bought on credit than remain simply to pay their outstanding debts to the company.[163] Scrip was used to the very last year of operations, but as Figure 1 clearly shows, more people with debts of every kind left the camp after 1940 than in any other period studied. Oscar Huber's ideas about debts and labor had become anachronisms once prosperity had returned to America.

The coal company also lost control of its employees as the people of Madrid became less isolated in American society. Many men and their sons had gone to war and realized that they could be something more than coal miners. The adage "once a miner, always a miner" no longer rang true after 1945. The men saw that new, improved roads could take anyone any place where there were better opportunities, higher wages and more modern advantages. Dozens of miners moved on to Albuquerque, where they contributed to that city's enormous growth in the post-war era. Only the oldest and least restless employees stayed behind, while newcomers often left in a matter of days.[164]

Washington also contributed to Madrid's decline in indirect ways. The federal government threatened to use military personnel in the mines if Oscar Huber was unable to avert a strike in 1944. A walkout would have badly damaged the Manhattan Project at a crucial stage of its development, for nothing could be done in Los Alamos without Madrid's coal for heat and electricity. Huber decided that he would rather deal with a small local union than with a distant government agency that might intervene in all affairs. The superintendent thus finally signed a UMW contract while the country was still at war.[165] Some argue that this was the beginning of the end for the little town, for the union "demanded too much and finally broke Madrid."[166] But one must take exception to this view. The local union was hardly radical in its demands and conditions in Madrid barely changed after 1944. Any increase in wages nevertheless hurt Huber's company since it could not raise the price of its coal and still hope to compete with more modern fuels in New Mexico. Profits dwindled as wages slowly increased and coal prices remained quite stable.[167] The union thus contributed to Madrid's demise, but it did not deliver the death blow to a town whose fate was already sealed.

Finally, conditions in the mines and the coal business in general caused men to leave Madrid in ever greater numbers. The town's deep shafts were no longer considered safe by many of the miners who remained in camp.[168] Workers continued to extract coal with hand tools as a steady decline in business prohibited the use of expensive, modern machinery.[169] The Albuquerque & Cerrillos Coal Company now lost one after another of its major customers, including Los Alamos in 1949. Los Alamos, like most communities and institutions in New Mexico, had switched to more modern fuels and had left Madrid with little business and no real future.[170] Simple economics helped to close Madrid as little effort was made to replace the employees who packed up and left town. The State Mine Inspector could report that only 68 coal miners remained in all of Santa Fe County by 1948.[171]

The end came in 1954 when the coal mines were closed down and those who had lingered on were dismissed by Huber.[172] Madrid had fallen victim to American technological and social change and no glowing corporate image or "slick talk" could save it now. In the spring of 1954 Oscar Huber put his coal company and its camp up for sale at a price of $250,000; an advertisement in the *Wall Street Journal* served as an epitaph of a kind. It read

Entire town.
200 houses, grade and high school, power house, general store, tavern, machine shop, mineral rights, 9000 acres, excellent climate, fine industrial location.[173]

Huber also advertised in several coal mining journals, but few investors seemed interested in buying the once-famous town. They did, however, offer many ideas about what Madrid might become. Some suggested that the camp could serve as a resort, while others thought it might be rebuilt as a retirement village. One promoter even planned to make the town into a movie set and tourist attraction. The list of suggested plans seemed endless, but while ideas were cheap, Madrid and the cost of its remodeling were not.[174] Five groups or individuals expressed some interest in the decade 1964 to 1974, but none could raise the money to pay for Madrid's inflated half-million-dollar price tag. The most serious offer of this kind had completely fallen through by August, 1974.[175] Despite the imaginative plans of ambitious promoters, Madrid remained a lonely ghost town.

Disappointed by these failures, the Huber family at last abandoned its efforts to sell Madrid as a single package. In February, 1975, the town's 150 standing buildings were put on the market to be sold individually. Oscar Huber's heir, Joe, thought that the property might be sold in about six months. It was gone in sixteen days.[176] The miners' old shacks were quickly purchased for between fifteen and seventy-five hundred dollars each. Most houses were bought by young people whose down payments equalled ten percent of cost or less.[177] Joe Huber hoped that Madrid's new citizens might have enough capital left over to rebuild the town if the price of their homes was kept low. Huber was correct; the rebuilding began almost immediately.[178] Madrid's population had declined to as little as two families in 1960 and equalled only a few renters in the early 1970s, but by May of 1975 the total grew to over eighty individuals.[179] Madrid's renaissance had begun.

The revitalized town has not, however, always enjoyed the glowing press coverage that Madrid received in the 1930s. A national magazine has dismissed the village as a "hippie enclave" where only "beads, belts, blouses and skirts" are made.[180] A New Mexican reporter reinforced this image by calling the people of Madrid "East Coast dropouts" who rely on welfare checks or rich benefactors in order to survive. According to that writer, "They are certainly pioneers of sorts but the cushion of a bank account back East knocks at the integrity of their experiment."[181]

Such criticism is hardly warranted. Most of the men and women of Madrid are self-sufficient, well-educated property owners who share a sincere interest in their new community. Some are forced to rely on welfare or have turned to their families for their initial capital investments, but the majority are economically independent and productive. Many are fine artists and musicians, while others run local shops or travel to Santa Fe or Albuquerque to earn their living.[182] At the time of this writing only one lot has been repossessed for failure to meet mortgage payments, and most residents have survived their first winter in town.[183]

Issues that involve the entire community are discussed in open town meetings. The citizens have organized a Landowners' Association to help solve common problems.[184] A volunteer fire department was formed and a cooperative school established in the old Catholic Church on the back street of town. In December, 1975, an effort was even made to revive Madrid's Christmas tradition on a small scale.[185] Other holidays have been celebrated by the community, and softball games are sometimes played in Madrid's ancient ball park.[186] The townspeople often gather in Vicki Van Deusan's general store and one couple have gone so far as to write "The Ballad of the Town of Madrid, New Mexico."[187] All now share in the enormous task of rebuilding Madrid's broken-down homes. While there is no longer an Employees Club in Madrid, the town's social isolation, informal institutions and pioneer life have done much to create a strong community spirit such as existed in the 1930s.

But Madrid is hardly a utopia. Its young citizens in fact face the same problems that have confronted many frontier communities in history. There is, for example, a serious shortage of water. Fires remain a constant danger in this dry region and one blaze claimed a life and burned a large garage on April 7, 1976.[188] A single eight-party telephone line connects Madrid with the outside world. The town's school, known as the Children's Workshop, lacks space and funds. Only thirty pupils can be taught in the old church, and Shelly Zang reports that "The monthly tuition of twenty-five dollars [per student] doesn't always pay even the teachers' salaries."[189] In early 1975 Madrid was also plagued by "gunslingers" from Cerrillos as they sped through town shooting in all directions.[190]

The people of Madrid are divided on what they wish their adopted town to become. There are two main factions of opinion. One group may be called the "isolationists," because they came to Madrid to create a new life away from the turmoil of modern society. These people are opposed to too much development and too many tourists in town. One young man expressed these feelings by declaring that "We just want to be left alone. I want Madrid to stay basically the same."[191] The speaker was rather annoyed by tourists roaming through town and recalled how at least one stranger started to walk off with his frying pan because the outsider thought the item was an antique. A second "isolationist" concluded that "Some day we may have to find another ghost town when things become too crowded."[192]

Another faction has less trepidation about growth and tourism and may therefore be called the "developers." Many in this group have

Christmas at Madrid was a major celebration until the early 40s. *Top:* Decorating the houses with *farolitos.*
Center: Boys with their Employees Club gifts on Christmas morning.
Bottom: Part of the Toyland set up at the ball park for Madrid's children and the many visitors.

Overleaf: The famous Christmas lights as seen in 1935. (Photographs from the Huber Papers.)

Top: The Madrid Miners baseball team was a source of pride for everyone in the community. Good semi-pro players often were hired for easy jobs in the mines. The team pictured is the 1929 Central New Mexico League champions. Bottom: Going out to the ball park to watch the team was a local pastime after a shift or on weekends. The team was one of the cohesive forces in the town. (Photographs from the Huber Papers.)

Although Madrid was renowned for its Christmas celebration, its citizens were almost as enthusiastic about the Fourth of July. *Top:* Mine Number 8's float for the Fourth. *Center:* A girls' foot race down the main street. *Bottom:* An Independence Day horse race. (Photographs from the Huber Papers.)

opened shops or joined a cooperative to market their art in a single gallery. These individuals anticipate a great economic boom in the near future, although no one wants Madrid to become a tourist trap where profits rule the course of life.[193] Many share a Black resident's confidence that the town will soon be "the next big Southwestern art center," as Taos and Santa Fe once were.[194] The group is simply interested in a controlled growth and a modest level of prosperity, if such things are still possible in the late twentieth century.[195]

But the issue of Madrid's future is quite minor in the town's everyday life. Cooperation rather than conflict and tolerance rather than division characterize the growing village. Life and labor have thus changed considerably since the Great Depression, and Oscar Huber would have difficulty recognizing his old coal camp. But Madrid is once again a close-knit and peaceful community removed from the mainstream of American life. Madrid is reborn.

• Notes •

1 *Kansas City Star,* December 17, 1939; *Raton Daily Range,* January 6, 1941; *Albuquerque Journal,* November 14, 1941.

2 *Los Angeles Evening Herald Express,* December 25, 1937; *Chicago Daily Tribune,* November 27, 1940; *New York Sunday Mirror,* December 15, 1940; *Miami Daily News,* December 22, 1940; *Ft. Worth Star-Telegram,* January 5, 1941; *Houston Chronicle,* November 30, 1941; *Denver Post,* December 21, 1941.

3 Interview, Claude Whipple, September 19, 1975. Whipple visited the town's Christmas in the late 1930s and worked on the "outside gang" at Madrid in 1948.

4 Editorial quoted in the *New Mexico Magazine,* XVII (January, 1939), 39.

5 Dr. M. D. Gibbs, "The Lights of Madrid," n.d., Oscar Huber Papers. The Huber Papers are deposited at the Eckerts Furniture Building, Albuquerque, New Mexico.

6 Quoted in Oscar Huber to George Kaseman, July 11, 1934, Madrid. Unless otherwise stated, all cited letters and telegrams sent between Huber and Kaseman are from the Huber Papers, with the former writing from Madrid and the latter writing from Albuquerque.

7 Huber to James B. Allen, June 17, 1962, Albuquerque, Huber Papers.

8 Interviews, George Salas, June 24, 1975 and Pedro Septulvida, July 10, 1975. Salas mined in Madrid from 1928 to 1935 and belonged to the UMW local. Septulvida mined from 1938 to 1947 and served as the local's president, 1946-47.

9 Interviews, Norman Thompson, July 10, 1975; Charles Franks, June 10, 1975; Julia Vergolio Weeks, June 26, 1975. Thompson was the weighboss at the tipple, 1936-42; Franks was a mine foreman in the late 1930s; Weeks was a school teacher, 1922-45.

10 Huber to Kaseman, June 14, 1932.

11 Interview, Margerie Lloyd, May 21, 1975. Mrs. Lloyd's husband, Lewis J. Lloyd, served as a clerk in Madrid, 1912-17 and 1933-43.

12 Huber to Kaseman, May 11, 1934; June 20, 1934; March 22, 1935; April 30, 1935; January 15, 1936.

13 Huber to Kaseman, November 22, 1933.

14   Huber to Kaseman, June 14, 1932.

15   Interviews, Jane Hustler, June 5, 1975 and Judge Harry E. Stowers, Jr., June 5, 1975. Mrs. Hustler's husband, Joseph Hustler, served as a clerk in Madrid in the 1930s; Judge Stowers' father played baseball and worked in the town in the same decade.

16   Interviews, Franks; Stowers; Johnny "Red" Garcia, June 4, 1975; William C. Brandenburg, September 14, 1976. Brandenburg played first base and the outfield for Madrid from 1930-40 while working as the boss at the power plant in town. The Miners also played annual exhibition games at the state penitentiary and against such professional teams as the House of David and the Detroit Giants. The former team was known for its players' beards in an age of clean-shaven males, while the latter club was manned by some of the most famous Black athletes of the era.

17   Interviews, Hustler; Mrs. J. D. Collister, May 15, 1975; Mr. and Mrs. Charles Gibbs, June 10, 1975. Mrs. Collister was Oscar Huber's oldest daughter; Mr. Gibbs was the manager of the company store in the 1930s. Also see *Albuquerque Journal*, n.d., Oscar Huber Papers, Scrapbook #9, p. 40.

18   Interviews, Johnny García; Joe Huber, June 3, 1975; *Raton Daily Range*, January 6, 1941. Joe Huber was Oscar Huber's only son; he ran the car dealership in Madrid. "Company men" included all employees except miners, but the term was sometimes used to describe individuals who were particularly faithful to the company.

19   Interviews, Thompson; Septulvida; Brandenburg; George Tabacchi, July 14, 1975. Tabacchi was the butcher in the company store.

20   Interviews, Johnny García and Franks.

21   Huber to Kaseman, June 14, 1932.

22   E. W. Bahr's letter to the editor, *Albuquerque Tribune*, December 30, 1936.

23   *New Mexico Magazine*, XVII (December, 1939), 20; Marcus Bach, "One Town's Christmas," *Christian Century* (December 18, 1940), 1581; *Newsweek*, XVI (December 30, 1940), 33; Carey Holbrook, "Christmas Comes to Madrid," *Compressed Air Magazine*, XLVI (December, 1941), 6603-06.

24   *Albuquerque Journal*, November 21, 1941. The company apparently shared most Employee Club expenses. In May, 1935, for example, Huber "made a deal between the Employees Club and ourselves to decorate the hall" before a special Saturday-night dance. Huber to Kaseman, May 15, 1935.

25   Interview, Weeks; *Kansas City Star*, December 17, 1939.

26   *Albuquerque Journal* and *Albuquerque Tribune*, December 13, 1938. Also, interview, Brandenburg.

27   *New Mexico Examiner*, December 15, 1938. On January 30, 1939, the New Mexico State Legislature passed House Joint Resolution #9 Commending the Citizens of Madrid, New Mexico, for their Magnificent Christmas Display. The resolution stated that "this spectacle has been

presented without any thought of gain or monetary return, but solely for the purpose of observing the season in a manner befitting a Christian Community." Oscar Huber Papers, Scrapbook #10.

28 Myra Ellen Jenkins to the author, Santa Fe, April 5, 1976. Jenkins is chief of the Historical Services Division in the State Records Center and Archives.

29 *Madrid Employees Club Bulletin,* December 25, 1940; *Albuquerque Journal,* December 15, 1937; interview, Gibbs.

30 Interviews, Franks; Gibbs; Stowers; García; J. Huber; Collister; Brandenburg.

31 U. S. Department of the Interior, Bureau of Mines, *Final Report of Mine Fire, Lamb Mine,* May 28 to June 2, 1934; interviews, J. Huber; Miguel Levya, June 3, 1975; John Peña, December 6, 1975. Levya was a miner, 1911-14, a merchant in Cerrillos, and a state legislator in the 1930s. Peña was born and raised in Madrid, 1932-49, and mined there, 1949-54.

32 Madrid was also plagued with occasional floods and mining disasters, but the latter were neither as frequent nor as fatal as in other coal regions of the state. Twenty-four men were killed in a Madrid mine explosion in 1896, while 14 lost their lives in 1922, 5 died in 1930 and 14 did not survive in 1932. *Albuquerque Tribune,* December 23, 1936. The total of all these tragic accidents did not, however, equal the 122 deaths in a single mine explosion in Dawson, New Mexico, in 1923.

33 Quoted in the *El Paso Times,* October 14, 1930.

34 Bach, "One Town's Christmas," 1,582. Also see Resolution #9, Note #27.

35 Huber to Kaseman, June 14, 1932.

36 *Ibid.*

37 Interview, Fay "Lefty" Webster, by Jim Boggio, n.d. Webster was a semi-professional outfielder who played for several teams in the Central New Mexico League. The author is grateful to Jim Boggio of KOAT-TV for his information on this and other interviews with former players of the league. Also, interview with Webster by author, June 21, 1976.

38 Interview, J. Huber, August 29, 1975.

39 *New Mexico Magazine,* XV (December, 1937), 8. Again see Resolution #9, Note #27.

40 Interview, Fremont Kutnewsky, May 19, 1975.

41 Fremont Kutnewsky, "Behind the Lights at Madrid," *New Mexico Magazine,* XXV (March, 1947), 33.

42 Myrtle Andrews, "Christmas in Madrid," *New Mexico Magazine,* XIV (December, 1936), 9 & 11.

43 *Albuquerque Journal,* n.d., Oscar Huber Papers, Scrapbook #9, p. 40.

44 R. H. Faxon to Huber, Raton, January 22, 1941, Huber Papers.

45 Frank Wilson's letter to the editor, *Santa Fe Sentinel,* January 26,

1940. Wilson was an organizer for the Workers' Alliance of Santa Fe and wrote this letter "as told to me by a Madrid miner." Also, interview, Peña.

46 Huber to Kaseman, November 22, 1933; interview, Gibbs. Carriers who brought the payroll from Albuquerque were often forced to change their routes to Madrid in order to avoid robberies. See Huber to Kaseman, August 28, 1933.

47 Huber to Kaseman, November 22, 1933; interviews, J. Huber; Johnny García.

48 Interview, Joseph Comisky, June 24, 1975. Comisky was a timberman and later an assistant foreman in the period 1925 to 1952.

49 Interviews, J. Huber; Comisky; Septulvida.

50 *Albuquerque Tribune,* December 16, 1941.

51 *Albuquerque Journal,* May 11, 1934; interviews, Gibbs; Levya; Septulvida; Salas; Joseph Longacre, July 14, 1975. Longacre was a roperider, 1927-32.

52 Margerie Lloyd, "This Was Madrid," *New Mexico Magazine,* XLII (November-December, 1964), 44; interviews, Lloyd; Gibbs.

53 Interviews, Weeks; Lloyd; Gibbs.

54 Interview, Thompson. Only star ballplayers or particularly valuable employees were free from such pressures. Interview, Brandenburg.

55 Interview, Thompson.

56 Interviews, J. Huber; Salas; Septulvida.

57 Interviews, J. Huber; Peña.

58 Huber to Kaseman, September 2, 1933.

59 Quoted in the *Albuquerque Journal,* May 11, 1934.

60 See William E. Leuchtenburg, *Franklin D. Roosevelt and the New Deal, 1932-40* (New York: Harper Torchbooks, 1963), pp. 106-107; Hugh Johnson, *The Blue Eagle from Egg to Earth* (Garden City, N. Y.: Doubleday, 1935).

61 Section 7a of the National Industrial Recovery Act should not be considered the *only* cause for unionization in Madrid but, as elsewhere, it was the major *immediate* impetus to renewed union activity. Low wages, poor working conditions and a desire to influence decisions that affected their economic fate may eventually have caused the miners to unionize, but Section 7a precipitated their action in 1933.

62 Chairman, Madrid Employees' Representation Plan, to Major John D. Moore, Madrid, November 25, 1933, Oscar Huber Papers. Moore served on the National Labor Board in 1933. On Huber's role in organizing the company union see Huber to Kaseman, April 25, 1934. "Old Mexican Mexicans" were miners who retained their Mexican citizenship.

63 Chairman, Madrid Employees' Representation Plan, to Moore, November 25, 1933.

64 Editorial, *Albuquerque Tribune,* November 15, 1933. Kaseman had quite a different idea about why the company union failed. He wrote

that "there is not the same incentive in the Company Union, because, in the regular labor organizations, there is lots of easy money and glory, which is not the same in a home institution." Kaseman to Huber, November 15, 1933.

65　See Kathy Levy, "The Gallup Coal Strike of 1933," Unpublished Ms.; Richard Stephenson, "The Use of Troops in Labor Disputes in New Mexico," (Unpublished M.A. thesis, University of New Mexico, 1952), Chapter V.

66　*Santa Fe New Mexican,* November 3, 1933; Telegram, Huber to Kaseman, November 3, 1933; Huber to Kaseman, November 3, 1933. For other NMU "invasions" see Huber to Kaseman, August 11, 1933; R. G. Warncke to Huber, August 15, 1933; Huber to Kaseman, September 4, 1933; Huber to Kaseman, October 31, 1933. Martha Roberts' speech of November 2 is included in the Huber Papers, Letter Box #1.

67　Huber to Kaseman, November 3, 4 & 8, 1933.

68　Huber to Kaseman, September 5, 1933; October 21, 1933; November 4, 1933; Stephenson, "Troops in Labor Disputes," 120-21. Also see Martha Roberts to Robert F. Roberts, Gallup, August 11, 1933, Oscar Huber Papers. "Bob" Roberts was in Madrid when he received this letter.

69　H. L. Taylor to Huber, August 15, 1933; Huber to Kaseman, October 16, 1933 and October 23, 1933. Taylor was Huber's chief clerk.

70　*Albuquerque Journal,* May 11, 1934; Huber to Kaseman, May 13, 1934. Also see Leuchtenburg, *Roosevelt and the New Deal,* p. 106.

71　The local union struck against the coal company on May 9-12, 1934; December 13-24, 1934; September 24-27, 1935; and January 31-March 2, 1936. Huber to Kaseman, May 9, 1934; Huber to Kaseman, December 13, 1934; *Albuquerque Journal,* May 11, 1934 and *Albuquerque Journal,* December 20, 1934, September 27, 1935; and all Huber-Kaseman correspondence from January 31 to March 2, 1936. Madrid's longest and most violent strike took place from April 28 to July 3, 1941. See *Albuquerque Journal,* November 10-14, 18, 19, 21, 1941 and *Santa Fe New Mexican,* May 25, 1941; November 9, 10, 12, 13-15, 18, 21, 22, 1941.

72　Interview, Thompson.

73　Telegram, Bill Zurek to Frank Hefferly, Cerrillos, February 2, 1936, Oscar Huber Papers. Hefferly was a regional leader of the UMW.

74　Taylor to Huber, January 31, 1936; Huber to Kaseman, February 3, 1936.

75　Huber to Kaseman, February 5, 1936; office memos and telegrams from Huber to Kaseman through the month of February compare the number of men at work and the number who appeared on picket lines each morning.

76　Wilson's letter to the editor, *Santa Fe Sentinel,* January 26, 1940.

77　Interviews, Levya; Salas, *Albuquerque Journal,* November 12, 1941. The men were also charged $1.25 for the Christmas tree they were required to keep in their front yards. Interviews, Septulvida; Peña;

Huber to Kaseman, January 29, 1936; Wilson's letter to editor, *Santa Fe Sentinel*, January 26, 1940.

Ibid.

79 Interview, Septulvida.

80 Huber to Kaseman, April 10 & 14, 1934.

81 Huber to Kaseman, August 28, 1933; March 1, 1934.

82 Interviews, Thompson; Tabacchi.

83 Huber to Kaseman, August 28, 1933; November 22, 1933; December 2, 1933; March 1, 1934.

84 Interviews, Lloyd; Gibbs.

85 Interviews, Lloyd; Salas; Peña.

86 Jesus Pallares quoted in the *Albuquerque Journal*, May 11, 1934. Also see the *Albuquerque Journal*, November 12, 1941; interviews, Peña; Manuel García, April 5, 1976. García mined in Madrid from 1936 to 1952.

87 Margery Wilson, "Madrid: Brief Analysis," 1935, New Mexico State Records Center and Archives. Wilson was a county welfare agent.

88 Over 100,000 gallons of water had to be transported into Madrid in railroad tank cars each day. The area was so dry that house fires had to be put out with the use of dynamite rather than water. Interviews, J. Huber; Hustler.

89 Interviews, Levya; Peña. Margaret McKittrick, "Lights Over Madrid, New Mexico," The McKittrick Papers, New Mexico State Records Center and Archives.

90 Wilson's letter to the editor, *Santa Fe Sentinel*, January 26, 1940. Also, interview, Peña.

91 Interviews, J. Huber; Thompson; Judge Stowers; Longacre. Bahr's letter to the editor, *Albuquerque Tribune,* December 30, 1936.

92 Huber to Allen, June 17, 1962. Interviews, J. Huber; Thompson; Hustler.

93 Huber to Allen, June 17, 1962; Interviews, J. Huber; Gibbs; Tabacchi; Brandenburg.

94 Interview, Weeks.

95 Interview, J. Huber.

96 Kaseman to Huber, October 25, 1935.

97 Interviews, Salas; Septulvida; Franks.

98 Interviews, Salas; Septulvida; Levya; Franks.

99 Few in town complained about Madrid's hospital and school, although fight wounds and frequent pregnancies were typically working class "ailments" and no adult education existed to teach literacy. Teachers were, moreover, never dismissed for their radical beliefs in the 1930s, but they were carefully screened when recruited so that union sympathizers need not have applied. Interviews, Weeks; Thompson; J. Huber.

100   Huber to Allen, June 17, 1962. Interviews, J. Huber; Gibbs; Tabacchi.

101   Quoted in the *Albuquerque Journal,* May 11, 1934.

102   Quoted in McKittrick, "Lights Over Madrid."

103   Madrid Supply Company Inventory, June 30, 1939, Albuquerque & Cerrillos Coal Company Records.

104   Interviews, Salas; Thompson.

105   See ads in the *Albuquerque Journal,* June 3, 1931; June 7, 1935; Kaseman to Huber, October 21, 1935. Also, interview, Manuel García.

106   Huber to Kaseman, May 29, 1935.

107   Taylor to Huber, January 23, 1935.

108   Huber to Kaseman, December 24, 1934; March 11, 1936; March 14, 1936. Huber also tried to get the union leader to leave town by finding work for him elsewhere in New Mexico. In the spring of 1935 Huber reported that a state agent "says he will do everything possible to get some sort of job for Zurek." Huber to Kaseman, March 27, 1935. Zurek was assigned to a "bridge gang" in Rio Arriba County in less than a month. The superintendent "arranged so that this information got to Mrs. Zurek as she has been anxious to get away and we felt that if she knew it Zurek would be less apt, or able, to back out." Huber to Kaseman, April 18, 1935. The company's plan fell through, although neither Huber nor Kaseman ever explained why.

109   According to the *New Mexican's* editorial of November 22, 1941, "The racketeers in the labor movement will destroy all gains made by labor. And the working man, not the fat-salaried labor leaders, will do the paying."

110   Quoted in Huber to Kaseman, February 24, 1936. "Blacklegs" were men who had originally struck but returned to work before the walkout ended. Union members constantly complained about "traitors and stool pigeons." See, for instance, Huber to Kaseman, June 22, 1935.

111   Huber to Kaseman, April 22 & 27, 1936; Taylor to Huber, April 29, 1936.

112   Huber to George Larson, January 20, 1939. Larson was an official of the Albuquerque & Cerrillos Coal Company.

113   Interview, Thompson.

114   Huber to Kaseman, March 2, 1936.

115   Huber to Kaseman, July 2, 1937.

116   The two men agreed to begin this correspondence on the "labor situation" in Huber to Kaseman, August 28, 1933, and Kaseman to Huber, August 30, 1933. Huber acquired ownership of the Albuquerque & Cerrillos Coal Company after Kaseman died in 1938.

117   When union organizers first met with the miners Huber wrote, "I felt that possibly it [would not be wise] to try to stop this meeting but to try and have some people present who would tell us what was going on and try to keep the meeting as quiet as possible." Huber to Kaseman, August 11, 1933. On information gathered by spies see R. G.

Warncke to Huber, August 15, 1933; Taylor to Huber, August 15, 1933; Huber to Kaseman, September 21, 1933; Taylor to Huber, May 18, 1934; Huber to Kaseman, August 17, 1934; February 8, 1936; April 22, 1936. Union leaders were aware of these spies but realized the advantages of not having to hold their meetings out of town. Huber to Kaseman, October 23, 1935. Also see the *Sunday Worker*, March 28, 1937, datelined Madrid.

118 Darling to Taylor, August 10, 1933. Huber was careful not to ask his informers questions that might create more problems than they solved. On October 19, 1935, he thus reported to Kaseman that the labor situation was "unusually quiet. We do not even hear any rumors one way or the other [about strikes] and, of course, don't want to start any by making too many inquiries."

119 Huber to Kaseman, February 24, 1935, and February 25, 1937.

120 Huber to Kaseman, November 17, 1934. Also see Huber to Kaseman, October 12, 1935.

121 See Huber to Kaseman, August 21, 1933; August 22, 1933; June 19, 1934; May 4, 1935; June 15, 1935; Huber to State Motor Vehicle Department, September 5, 1933 and August 20, 1934.

122 See Kaseman to Huber, January 30, 1935; George Miksch to Huber, Gallup, November 13, 1935; Taylor to Huber, November 18, 20, 21 and 22, 1933, and Huber to Kaseman, December 2, 1933; Hustler to Huber, September 1, 1933; Archie Danford to Kaseman, Trinidad, Colorado, June 2, 1934; Huber to Kaseman, January 5, 1935.

123 Quoted in the *Albuquerque Tribune,* April 28, 1941.

124 Huber to Kaseman, May 24 & 25, 1934. A black member of the union was later discharged when the company doctor disqualified him for "defective eyes." *Albuquerque Journal*, November 19, 1941.

125 Huber to Kaseman, May 3 & 13, 1934 and June 7, 1934.

126 Huber to Kaseman, July 22, 1935.

127 Huber to Kaseman, October 27, 1933 and February 6, 1936. Pallares was deported to Mexico in 1935. See Huber to Kaseman, May 25, 1935. Kaseman never thought that the government was doing enough in deporting other foreign radicals. He wrote that "it is hard for any one to realize, who has not been thoroughly posted and repeatedly told, how pro-foreign our government is, and the obstructions that exist in the way of deporting any one or even discriminating between native and foreign agitators." Kaseman to Huber, February 11, 1936.

128 A. B. Jaliana to Huber, Gallup, August 9, 1933; Huber to Kaseman, November 9, 1933; Telegram, Kaseman to D. Roberts, May 14, 1934. D. Roberts was the sheriff in Gallup.

129 Huber to Kaseman, June 8, 1936.

130 Telegrams, Huber to Romolo Lopez, February 13, 1936, 9:35 a.m.; Romolo Lopez to Huber, February 15, 1936, 11:32 a.m.

131 Huber to Kaseman, March 17, 1936.

132 Kaseman to Huber, November 16, 1933. Also see Kaseman to Huber, November 27, 1933.

133   Huber to Kaseman, September 6, 1933; Kaseman to Huber, January 6, 1935.

134   Huber to Kaseman, August 16, 1936.

135   Huber to Kaseman, June 20, 1934 and March 27, 1936.

136   Wilson, "Brief Analysis."

137   Huber to Kaseman, August 24, 1937.

138   Huber gave the following information on Madrid's profits and losses:

1934	$ 1,154.91 profit
1935	$ 7,582.18 loss
1936	$24,251.82 loss
1937	$18,195.40 loss
1938	$ 4,134.46 profit
1939	$ 831.17 loss

Albuquerque Journal, November 22, 1941. According to these figures the coal company sustained a total loss of $45,571.20 in the period 1934-39.

139   Kaseman nevertheless wrote Huber to "be careful not to say anything that might be construed. . .that you would sign. . .a contract with the United Mine Workers, even if they had practically all of our employees signed up." Kaseman to Huber, May 10, 1935.

140   Kaseman made these charges in the *Albuquerque Journal,* May 11, 1934, and Huber agreed in many letters, including Huber to Kaseman, November 29, 1933; September 27, 1935; October 30, 1935; February 11, 1936.

141   Huber to Kaseman, March 20, 1936.

142   Huber to Kaseman, March 12, 1936. 107 of the voters had left town while 21 were not working or picketing. Huber assumed that women voters would vote the same way as their husbands.

143   Interviews, Septulvida; Levya. Also see E. R. Harrington, "Desert Gold," *New Mexico Magazine,* XVII (November, 1939), 10, 11, 37, 38.

144   Interview, Gibbs.

145   Wilson, "Brief Analysis." There were about 225 families in Madrid in 1935.

146   Interview, Comisky; J. Huber.

147   Huber to Kaseman, April 14, 1934; May 13, 1934; August 24, 1937. Also see Kaseman to Huber, July 21, 1934.

148   Huber to Miksch, May 1, 1936. Also see Huber to Kaseman, October 17, 1935. Huber later served on the State Welfare Board. *Albuquerque Journal,* November 12, 1941.

149   Huber to Kaseman, April 12, 1935.

150   Interviews, Thompson; Weeks; Peña.

151   Interview, Hustler.

152   *U. S. Bureau of Mines Report,* 1932; Huber to Kaseman, April 9, 1937.

153   Interviews, Gibbs; Stowers; Margaret García, June 10, 1975. Margaret García was raised in Madrid in the 1930s.

154   *Santa Fe New Mexican,* November 8, 1941.

155   Quoted in *ibid.*

156   Interview, J. Huber, May 19, 1976. Also, author's telephone conversation with Dan Smith, June 19, 1975. On that date Smith presented a television documentary on conditions in Los Alamos during World War II.

157   Interviews, J. Huber, June 3, 1975 and May 19, 1976; Manuel García.

158   *Report of the State Mine Inspector of New Mexico* (Santa Fe: New Mexico State Printing Office, 1941, 1943 & 1945).

159   Natalie White, "What Became of the Southwest's Christmas City?" *Desert Magazine,* XXIV (December, 1961), 31.

160   Interviews, Whipple; Peña.

161   Interviews, Manuel García; Whipple.

162   Interview, J. Huber, May 19, 1976.

163   Interview, Manuel García.

164   *Ibid.*

165   Interviews, J. Huber, June 3, 1975, and May 19, 1976.

166   Interviews, Thompson; Hustler.

167   Interview, J. Huber, May 19, 1976.

168   Interview, Manuel García.

169   Interviews, J. Huber, May 19, 1976, and E. C. Beaumont, May 21, 1976. Beaumont is a geologist who has studied Madrid's mineral resources and the problem of mining in the area. He contends that only an urgent demand for energy sources would make the expense of mining in Madrid a profitable venture.

170   Interview, J. Huber, May 19, 1976.

171   *Report of the State Mine Inspector of New Mexico* (Santa Fe: New Mexico State Printing Office, 1948).

172   Only a skeleton crew was kept on for about three years in order to salvage old equipment for resale in the coal industry.

173   *Wall Street Journal,* June 17, 1954.

174   Interview, J. Huber, May 19, 1976.

175   *Ibid.*

176   Interview, Robert Dunbar, May 20, 1976. Dunbar was one of the three real estate agents who sold Madrid's homes. He is a partner in the Sierra Madre Realty Company which still owns several buildings in town. Oscar Huber died in 1962.

177   *Ibid.*

178   Interviews, J. Huber, May 19, 1976, and Dunbar. Dunbar has, however, resold houses for three times their original price once they were improved. Land speculation is common as the price of property has increased with the town's growth.

179   Interview, J. Huber, May 19, 1976; *Albuquerque Tribune*, May 24, 1975. Shacks were rented for as little as ten to fifteen dollars per month in the early 1970s. Renters were given the option to buy their homes when the buildings were put on sale and 29 of the 30 tenants did so. Interview, J. Huber, May 19, 1976.

180   *Family Circle*, May, 1976, 198.

181   *Seers Catalogue*, October 4-17, 1975. More sympathetic views of Madrid have appeared in the *New York Times*, August 9, 1975, and the *Albuquerque Tribune*, May 24, 1975.

182   Interview, Francie Rosen, April 12, 1976. Rosen and her husband currently own the Packrat's Nest shop in Madrid.

183   Interview, J. Huber, May 19, 1976.

184   Interview, Terry Conrad, June 3, 1975. Conrad, an artist, owns the old Lamb Hotel in Madrid.

185   *Santa Fe New Mexican*, December 21, 1975; interview, Rosen.

186   *Santa Fe New Mexican*, November 2, 1975, and *New York Times*, August 9, 1975.

187   Larry and Francie Lee's ballad appeared in the *Santa Fe New Mexican*, December 7, 1975. Lee is the Rosens' pen name.

188   *Albuquerque Journal*, April 8, 1976; interview, Conrad, April 9, 1976.

189   Correspondence, Shelly Zang to the author, Madrid, May 11, 1976. Zang and Dennis Dunnum are the Workshop's teachers. The school receives a book allowance from the state, but the teachers must still raise much of their funds from benefits held in town.

190   Interview, Rosen.

191   Anonymous individual quoted in *Seers Catalogue*, October 4-17, 1975.

192   *Ibid.*

193   Interview, Rosen.

194   Roszel Scott quoted in the *New York Times*, August 9, 1975.

195   These hopes are already mixed with some fears because outsiders have leased space in Madrid's old company store and have begun to sell their wares. Some "developers" resent this practice which takes money out of town. The Sierra Madre Real Estate Company, which rents the space, claims that most of the outsiders do not compete with local merchants because the former sell goods that are not otherwise available in Madrid. The company also argues that the extra stops attract more tourists who in turn spend more money in all of Madrid's stores. Interviews, Rosen; Dunbar.

• Bibliography •

PRIMARY SOURCES

Archives and Records

Albuquerque & Cerrillos Coal Company Records, Eckerts Furniture Building, Albuquerque, New Mexico.

Madrid Employees Club Bulletins.

The Oscar Huber Papers, Eckerts Furniture Building, Albuquerque, New Mexico.

The Margaret McKittrick Papers, State Records Center & Archives, Santa Fe, New Mexico.

Report of the State Mine Inspector of New Mexico. Santa Fe: State Printing Office, 1912-54.

Interviews and Correspondence

E. C. Beaumont, May 21, 1976.
William C. Brandenburg, September 14, 1976.
Mrs. J. D. Collister, May 15, 1975.
Joseph Comisky, June 24, 1975.
Terry Conrad, June 3, 1975; April 9, 1976.
Robert Dunbar, May 20, 1976.
Charles Franks, June 10, 1975.
Johnny "Red" García, June 4, 1975.
Manuel García, April 5, 1976.
Margaret García, June 10, 1975.
Mr. and Mrs. Charles Gibbs, June 6, 1975.
Joe Huber, June 3, July 22, August 29, 1975; May 19, 1976.
Jane Hustler, June 5, 1975.
Fremont Kutnewsky, May 19, 1975.
Miguel Levya, June 3, 1975.
Margerie Lloyd, May 21, 1975.
Joseph Longacre, July 14, 1975.
Juan Peña, December 6, 1975.
Francie Rosen, April 12, 1976.
George Salas, June 24, 1975.
Pedro Septulvida, July 10, 1975.

Judge Harry E. Stowers, Jr., June 5, 1975.
Mr. and Mrs. George Tabacchi, July 14, 1975.
Norman Thompson, July 10, 1975.
Fay "Lefty" Webster, June 21, 1976.
Julia Vergolio Weeks, June 26, 1975.
Claude Whipple, September 19, 1975.
Shelly Zang to the author, Madrid, May 11, 1976.

Newspapers

Albuquerque Journal, 1930-41, 1975.
Albuquerque Tribune, 1930-41.
Chicago Daily Tribune, 1940.
Denver Post, 1941.
El Paso Times, 1930.
Ft. Worth Star-Telegram, 1941.
Gallup Independent, 1933.
Houston Chronicle, 1941.
Kansas City Star, 1939.
Los Angeles Evening Herald Express, 1937.
Miami Daily News, 1940.
New Mexico Examiner, 1938.
New York Sunday Mirror, 1940.
New York Times, 1975.
Raton Daily Range, 1941.
Santa Fe New Mexican, 1930-41, 1975.
Santa Fe Sentinel, 1940.
Seers Catalogue, 1975.
Socorro Chieftain, 1934.
Sunday Worker, 1937.

SECONDARY SOURCES

Allen, James B. *The Company Town in the American West*. Norman: University of Oklahoma Press, 1966.
Allen, Kenneth. "Christmas in the Mining Country." *Children's Friend*, XXV (December 21, 1941).
Andrews, Myrtle. "Christmas in Madrid." *New Mexico Magazine*, XIV (December, 1936), 9-11, 43.
Bach, Marcus. "One Town's Christmas." *Christian Century* (December, 1940), 1581-82.
"Company Stores and the Scrip System." *Monthly Labor Review*, XLI (July, 1935), 45-53.
Florin, Lambert. *New Mexico and Texas Ghost Towns*. Seattle: Superior Publishing Co., 1971.
Grady, Anne. "Oscar Huber: Profile." *Albuquerque Review*, II (July 13, 1962), 2.
Harrington, E. R. "Desert Gold." *New Mexico Magazine*, XVII (November, 1939), 10, 11, 37, 38.
Holbrook, Carey. "Christmas Comes to Madrid." *Compressed Air Mag-*

azine, XLVI (December, 1941), 6603-06.

Huber, Joe. *The Story of Madrid*. Albuquerque: Southwest Printing Co., 1963.

Jenkinson, Michael. *Ghost Towns of New Mexico*. Albuquerque: University of New Mexico Press, 1967.

Johnson, Hugh. *The Blue Eagle from Egg to Earth*. Garden City, N. Y.: Doubleday, 1935.

Johnson, Ole S. *The Industrial Store: Its History, Operations and Economic Significance*. Atlanta: University of Georgia Press, 1952.

Johnson, Virginia B. "Economic Aspects of National Regulation of the Bituminous Coal Industry, 1933-43." Unpublished M. A. Thesis. University of West Virginia, 1950.

Kutnewsky, Fremont. "Behind the Lights at Madrid." *New Mexico Magazine*, XXV (March, 1947), 33-39.

Leuchtenburg, William E. *Franklin D. Roosevelt and the New Deal, 1932-40*. New York: Harper Torchbooks, 1963.

Levy, Kathy. "The Gallup Coal Strike of 1933." Unpublished Ms.

Lloyd, Margerie. "This Was Madrid." *New Mexico Magazine*, XLII (November-December, 1964), 14-16.

Marshall, Jim. "Canyon Christmas." *Collier's* (December 20, 1941), 13.

Morris, Homer Lawrence. *The Plight of the Bituminous Coal Miner*. Philadelphia: University of Pennsylvania Press, 1934.

Morris, Thomas J. "The Coal Camp: A Pattern of Limited Community Life." Unpublished M. A. Thesis, University of West Virginia, 1950.

Motto, Sytha. *Madrid and Christmas in New Mexico* (n.p., 1973).

Sherman, James E. & Barbara H. *Ghost Towns and Mining Camps of New Mexico*. Norman: University of Oklahoma Press, 1975.

Stephenson, Richard. "The Use of Troops in Labor Disputes in New Mexico." Unpublished M. A. Thesis, University of New Mexico, 1952.

Van Kleeck, Mary. *Miners and Management*. New York: Russell Sage Foundation, 1934.

White, Natalie. "What Became of the Southwest's 'Christmas City'?" *Desert Magazine*, XXIV (December, 1961), 30-32.